LE CORDON BLEU

HOME COLLECTION

·CHOCOLATE·

MURDOCH BOOKS®

Sydney • London • Vancouver • New York

contents

recipe ratings ✱ *easy* ✱✱ *a little more care needed* ✱✱✱ *more care needed*

Flourless chocolate cake

Served with Chantilly cream and a sprinkling of flaked almonds, this dense chocolate cake makes a lovely dessert, but is perfect for a little chocolate indulgence on any occasion.

Preparation time **30 minutes**
Total cooking time **50 minutes**
Serves 8

150 g (5 oz) soft light brown sugar
225 g (7¼ oz) unsalted butter, softened
4 eggs, separated
200 g (6½ oz) good-quality dark chocolate,
coarsely grated
230 g (7¼ oz) ground almonds
2½ tablespoons caster sugar
2 tablespoons flaked almonds

CHANTILLY CREAM
300 ml (10 fl oz) cream, for whipping
few drops of vanilla extract or essence
2 tablespoons icing sugar

1 Lightly grease a 23 cm (9 inch) round cake tin and line the base with greaseproof paper. Preheat the oven to slow 150°C (300°F/Gas 2).

2 Cream the brown sugar and butter together in a large bowl until light and pale. Beat in the egg yolks one at a time, beating well after each addition. Stir in the chocolate and ground almonds until well combined. In a separate bowl, whisk the egg whites until stiff, whisk in the caster sugar, then fold it carefully into the chocolate mixture in four additions. Do not overfold, or the mixture will lose its volume. When there are no more streaks of white through the chocolate mixture, pour into the tin and bake for 50 minutes, or until it springs back when lightly touched in the centre. Cool the cake completely before removing it from the tin.

3 To make the Chantilly cream, whisk the cream with the vanilla and sugar in a large bowl until it is standing in stiff peaks. Keep chilled until needed.

4 To serve, cut the cake into wedges and serve with the Chantilly cream and a sprinkling of the flaked almonds.

Chef's tips This cake can be baked in a square tin for an alternative presentation to wedges.

You can grate the chocolate quickly by using the grater attachment of a food processor.

Chocolate profiteroles

*The name profiterole is derived from the French word 'profit', and originally meant
a small gift, which is just what these chocolate-smothered pastry balls are.*

*Preparation time **30 minutes***
*Total cooking time **30 minutes***

Serves 6

PROFITEROLES
1 teaspoon caster sugar
generous pinch of salt
100 g (3 1/4 oz) unsalted butter
125 g (4 oz) strong or plain flour, sifted
4 eggs, lightly beaten
1 egg, lightly beaten and strained, to glaze

FILLING
350 ml (11 fl oz) cream, for whipping
1 1/2 tablespoons caster sugar
1–2 drops vanilla extract or essence

icing sugar, to dust
Chocolate sauce, to serve (see page 60 for the recipe)

1 To make the profiteroles, preheat the oven to moderately hot 200°C (400°F/Gas 6). Brush a baking tray with melted butter and refrigerate until needed. Put 250 ml (8 fl oz) water with the sugar, salt and butter in a deep saucepan, bring to the boil and remove from the heat. Immediately add all the flour to the liquid and stir with a wooden spoon. Return the pan to low heat and cook, stirring continuously, until the mixture rolls off the sides of the pan. Remove from the heat and allow to cool until lukewarm. (If it is too hot the eggs will cook when they are added.) Gradually add the eggs, a little at a time, beating well between each addition. The mixture loosens with each addition, but thickens with beating. Stop adding the eggs once the mixture drops freely from the spoon. Spoon into a piping bag fitted with a 9 mm (3/8 inch) plain nozzle.

2 With the nozzle about 1 cm (1/2 inch) above the tray, pipe well-spaced rounds 2.5 cm (1 inch) in diameter, then stop the pressure on the bag and quickly pull away. Brush the top of each round with the strained egg, making sure that it does not run down the sides as it will burn during cooking. Lightly press down the top of each ball with the back of a fork to ensure an even shape when rising. Bake for 15–20 minutes, or until well risen and golden brown. The profiteroles should sound hollow when the base is tapped. Make a small hole in the base of each profiterole using the point of a small knife. Transfer to a wire rack to cool thoroughly.

3 To make the filling, whisk the cream, sugar and vanilla together until stiff peaks form. Spoon the cream into a piping bag fitted with a small round nozzle and pipe into the base of each profiterole.

4 To serve, stack the profiteroles in a pyramid in a glass bowl or on individual plates. Dust lightly with sifted icing sugar and serve with the warm chocolate sauce.

White chocolate crème brûlée

Hidden beneath the crackly sugar topping lies a creamy, white chocolate custard. The two textures combine beautifully to create this delicious variation of the traditional crème brûlée.

Preparation time **10 minutes + refrigeration**
Total cooking time **25 minutes**
Serves 6

400 ml (12³/4 fl oz) thick (double) cream
1 vanilla pod
130 g (4¹/4 oz) good-quality white chocolate, chopped
6 egg yolks
80 g (2³/4 oz) demerara sugar

1 Pour the cream into a medium saucepan. Split the vanilla pod lengthways and scrape out the seeds using the tip of a small pointed knife. Add the seeds and the pod to the cream and heat slowly until just at boiling point, over low to medium heat, allowing the flavour to infuse. Remove from the heat.

2 Put the chocolate in a bowl. Half fill a saucepan with water and bring to the boil. Remove from the heat and place the bowl over the pan, making sure it is not touching the water. Leave the chocolate to melt slowly, then remove the bowl from the pan. Stir in the yolks until well combined, then stir in the hot cream.

3 Pour this mixture into a clean saucepan and return to the stove over low heat. Stir constantly, with a wooden spoon, to prevent the mixture burning on the base of the pan. Continue to cook until the mixture thickens and coats the back of a spoon. Remove from the heat and strain through a fine sieve, discarding the vanilla pod. Pour the mixture into six 8 x 4 cm (3 x 1¹/2 inch), 120 ml (4 fl oz) ramekins, and set aside to cool. Refrigerate for several hours or overnight, or until they are firmly set.

4 Finish the crème brûlée by sprinkling with the sugar and placing under a hot grill until the sugar turns dark golden brown. Do not add the topping more than 2 hours before serving. Serve chilled.

Chef's tips Crème brûlée can be prepared in advance, to the end of step 3.

For an alternative topping, divide 80 g (2³/4 oz) of melted bittersweet chocolate evenly among the ramekins.

Chocolate fondue

Tradition states that if you drop your fruit into the fondue you must kiss the person opposite you.

Preparation time **15 minutes**
Total cooking time **10 minutes**
Serves 4

300 ml (10 fl oz) cream
50 ml (1 3/4 fl oz) milk
1 vanilla pod
500 g (1 lb) good-quality dark chocolate,
  finely chopped
1 banana
3 apples
3–4 slices fresh or canned pineapple
150 g (5 oz) strawberries

1 Place the cream and milk in a small saucepan. Split the vanilla pod lengthways and scrape the seeds into the pan. Add the vanilla pod to the pan. Slowly heat until just at boiling point. Remove from the heat, discard the vanilla pod and stir in the chocolate. Keep the chocolate fondue warm by sitting the pan within a larger pan of hand-hot water.
2 Cut the fruit into large slices or chunks, depending on the type of fruit. Leave the strawberries whole.
3 To serve, skewer a mixture of fruits for each person and serve with a small dish of fondue on each individual plate. Alternatively, serve the fondue in the centre of the table with the fruit and allow each person to dip one piece of fruit at a time into the fondue.

Chef's tip Vary your fruit selection to take advantage of each season.

Chocolate terrine

Even a small slice of this terrine is guaranteed to have you suffering from a chocolate overdose. The milk and dark chocolate mousse is surrounded with a layer of sponge cake, and topped with a rich chocolate coating.

Preparation time **1 hour + refrigeration**
Total cooking time **15 minutes**
Serves 10–12

GENOESE SPONGE
4 eggs
120 g (4 oz) caster sugar
80 g (2³/4 oz) plain flour
1¹/2 tablespoons cocoa powder

MILK CHOCOLATE MOUSSE
300 ml (10 fl oz) thick (double) cream
150 g (5 oz) good-quality milk chocolate, chopped
2 tablespoons caster sugar
2 egg yolks

DARK CHOCOLATE MOUSSE
300 ml (10 fl oz) thick (double) cream
150 g (5 oz) good-quality dark chocolate, chopped
2 tablespoons caster sugar
2 egg yolks

CHOCOLATE COATING
250 ml (8 fl oz) milk
300 g (10 oz) good-quality dark chocolate, chopped
75 g (2¹/2 oz) caster sugar

1 To make the Genoese sponge, preheat the oven to moderately hot 200°C (400°F/Gas 6). Line two 25 x 30 cm (10 x 12 inch) swiss roll tins with baking paper. Put the eggs and sugar in a large bowl and place over a pan of barely steaming water. Whisk with electric beaters for 5–7 minutes, or until the mixture is thick and creamy, and has doubled in volume. The mixture should never be hot, only warm. Remove the bowl from the pan and whisk until cold. Sift the flour and cocoa together, and carefully fold into the egg mixture. Stop folding as soon as the flour and cocoa are just combined. Pour into the tins and bake on the middle shelf of the oven for 5–6 minutes, or until springy and shrinking from the paper. Turn out onto a wire rack. Put another rack on top, turn over, remove the top rack and leave to cool, then peel away the paper. Trim the sponge and use it to line a 19 x 9 x 7 cm (7¹/2 x 3¹/2 x 2³/4 inch), 1.75 litre terrine mould. Reserve a slice 19 x 9 cm (7¹/2 x 3¹/2 inches) to fit on top of the terrine.

2 To make the milk chocolate mousse, whisk the cream in a large bowl until it leaves a trail as it falls from the whisk. Put the chocolate in a bowl. Half fill a saucepan with water and bring to the boil. Remove from the heat and place the bowl over the pan, making sure it is not touching the water. Leave the chocolate to melt slowly, then remove the bowl from the pan. Dissolve the sugar in 45 ml (1¹/2 fl oz) water in a small saucepan over low heat and bring to the boil. Put the egg yolks in a small bowl and begin to whisk them. Pour on the bubbling syrup and whisk continuously until the mixture is thick and cold. Add to the chocolate and mix quickly to combine. Do not overmix. Add the whipped cream and carefully fold in with a plastic spatula or metal spoon.

3 To make the dark chocolate mousse, repeat step 2, replacing the milk chocolate with the dark chocolate.

4 Pour the milk chocolate mousse into the mould, smooth the surface with the back of a spoon, then pour in the dark chocolate mousse. Cover with the reserved sponge and freeze for 1 hour or refrigerate for 2 hours.

5 To make the coating, heat the milk until just at boiling point. Add to the chocolate and mix well. Dissolve the sugar in 75 ml (2¹/2 fl oz) water and bring to the boil. Add to the chocolate. Remove the terrine from the freezer and turn onto a wire rack. Lay a plate under the rack and pour the coating over the terrine. Transfer to a clean plate and serve at room temperature.

Chocolate ice cream cups

The history of ice cream dates back thousands of years where it began as a form of sorbet made of snow and honey. While this rich chocolate ice cream bears little resemblance to its humble ancestor, it is just as much of a delicacy. And, unlike the ancient sorbet, this ice cream can be enjoyed even when the snow isn't falling.

*Preparation time **20 minutes + overnight freezing***
*Total cooking time **10 minutes***
Serves 4–6

500 ml (16 fl oz) milk
1/2 vanilla pod, split lengthways
100 g (3 1/4 oz) good-quality dark chocolate, chopped
4 egg yolks
100 g (3 1/4 oz) caster sugar

CHOCOLATE CUPS
400 g (12 3/4 oz) good-quality dark chocolate, chopped

1 Put the milk, vanilla pod and chopped chocolate in a saucepan and heat slowly until just at boiling point. Remove from the heat. Prepare a large bowl of iced water. Whisk the egg yolks and caster sugar together until thick and pale. Pour in a third of the hot milk, blend and add to the pan with the rest of the milk. Cook over medium heat very slowly, stirring constantly, until the mixture thickens and coats the back of a spoon. When a finger is drawn across the coating the line should not close over the spoon again. Do not allow to boil, or the eggs will overcook and the mixture will separate. Cool the mixture as quickly as possible by putting the pan straight into the bowl of iced water. Strain into a jug.

2 Pour the mixture into an ice cream machine and churn for 15 minutes, or until set. The ice cream will be soft and may be served now or spooned into a 1 litre container and frozen until firm. If you do not have an ice cream machine, pour the strained mixture into a 1 litre container and freeze until just firm. Transfer to a large bowl and beat with electric beaters until thick and pale. Return to the container, cover and freeze until firm. Beat once more before pouring back into the container and freezing overnight.

3 To make the chocolate cups, follow the method in the Chef's techniques on page 63. When the cups are set, fill with scoops of the ice cream and serve. Delicious served with a fruit coulis or fresh fruit.

Cinnamon and chocolate chip biscuits

If one of these sweet little biscuits is delicious on its own, won't they be twice as delicious when two of them are sandwiched together with raspberry jam?

Preparation time **15 minutes + 20 minutes refrigeration**
Total cooking time **10–15 minutes**
Makes about 30

2 egg yolks
I teaspoon vanilla extract or essence
150 g (5 oz) unsalted butter, softened
100 g (3¹/4 oz) icing sugar
300 g (10 oz) plain flour
¹/2 teaspoon baking powder
generous pinch of salt
1¹/2 teaspoons ground cinnamon
80 g (2³/4 oz) chocolate chips
150 g (5 oz) raspberry jam

1 In a small bowl, lightly mix together the egg yolks, vanilla and 30 ml (1 fl oz) water. In a large bowl, using electric beaters or a wooden spoon, cream together the butter and icing sugar until pale and light. Gradually add the yolk mixture.

2 Sift together the flour, baking powder, salt and cinnamon, and add to the butter mixture. Stir until the flour is almost incorporated, then add the chocolate chips. Do not overwork the mixture. Using a hand, draw the mixture together into a rough ball of dough, wrap in plastic wrap and refrigerate for at least 20 minutes. Preheat the oven to moderate 180°C (350°F/Gas 4).

3 Roll the dough out on a lightly floured surface to a thickness of 4 mm (¹/4 inch). Cut out rounds with a 3 cm (1¹/4 inch) plain cutter, place on a baking tray and bake for 10–15 minutes, or until lightly golden brown. Remove from the tray and cool on a wire rack.

4 Spread the base of one biscuit with the raspberry jam and attach it to the base of another to make a sandwich. Continue until all the biscuits are sandwiched.

Chef's tip The unfilled biscuits will keep in an airtight container for up to a week. Once filled, their storage life is lessened to 1 or 2 days.

Chocolate brownies

The aroma of a batch of brownies baking may be irresistible, but it doesn't compare with the sensation of sinking your teeth into the finished product. The thick chocolate topping makes these twice as indulgent.

Preparation time **20 minutes + refrigeration**
Total cooking time **50 minutes**
Makes about 16

200 g (6¹/2 oz) unsalted butter, softened
3 teaspoons vanilla extract or essence
200 g (6¹/2 oz) caster sugar
50 g (1³/4 oz) good-quality dark chocolate, chopped
2 eggs, lightly beaten
100 g (3¹/4 oz) plain flour
pinch of salt
1 teaspoon baking powder
200 g (6¹/2 oz) walnuts, roughly chopped

TOPPING
100 ml (3¹/4 fl oz) thick (double) cream
100 g (3¹/4 oz) good-quality dark chocolate, chopped
40 g (1¹/4 oz) unsalted butter, softened

1 Grease a shallow 20 cm (8 inch) square baking tin, and sprinkle with flour or line the base with baking paper. Cream the butter, vanilla extract or essence and sugar together in a large bowl with a wooden spoon or electric beaters, until the mixture is light and fluffy.

Preheat the oven to warm 170°C (325°F/Gas 3).
2 Put the chocolate in a bowl. Half fill a saucepan with water and bring to the boil. Remove from the heat and place the bowl over the pan, making sure it is not touching the water. Leave the chocolate to melt slowly, then remove the bowl from the pan.
3 Gradually add the eggs to the creamed butter in about six additions, beating well after each addition, then stir in the melted chocolate.
4 Sift together the flour, salt and baking powder into a bowl, and add the chopped walnuts. Add to the chocolate mixture, and stir until just combined. Pour into the tin and bake for about 45 minutes, or until firm and springy to the touch of a finger. Cool in the tin.
5 To make the topping, pour the cream into a small saucepan and heat until just at boiling point. Remove from the heat and add the chocolate. Stir to melt, then whisk in the butter. Transfer to a bowl and refrigerate until cooled and slightly thickened before spreading on top of the brownies. Refrigerate until the topping is just set. Cut into squares to serve.

Chef's tips Use pecans in place of walnuts.
The brownies are superbly moist and will keep in an airtight container for up to a week.

False truffles

While the outside may deceive you into mistaking these for ordinary truffles, false truffles are far more wicked—balls of chocolate ice cream, smothered with rich chocolate ganache and rolled in cocoa.

Preparation time **30 minutes + 1 hour freezing**
Total cooking time **5 minutes**
Makes 12

250 ml (8 fl oz) chocolate ice cream
cocoa powder, to dust

GANACHE
250 g (8 oz) good-quality dark chocolate, chopped
250 ml (8 fl oz) thick (double) cream
2¹/₂ tablespoons caster sugar

1 Line a baking tray with baking paper. Scoop 12 small balls from the ice cream using a melon baller or a teaspoon. Place on the tray and freeze for at least 1 hour.
2 To make the ganache, put the chocolate in a bowl. Put the cream and sugar in a medium pan, and stir over low heat until the sugar has dissolved. Pour the cream mixture over the chocolate and leave it to melt for a few minutes, then gently stir until smooth. Keep stirring every 10 minutes for about 1 hour, or until cool.
3 Sift the cocoa powder into a shallow bowl. Once the balls of ice cream are frozen solid, remove a few at a time. Dip into the cooled ganache and immediately roll in the cocoa powder. Return to the freezer and repeat with the remaining balls.

Chef's tips The ganache must not be warm or it will melt the ice cream, nor must it be too cold or it will be too thick to coat properly.

Once they are frozen, the finished truffles may be kept in an airtight freezer bag for up to 1 month. Roll again in cocoa powder before serving, if necessary.

Chocolate sorbet

One scoop of this rich sorbet should be sufficient for most, but rarely is for true chocaholics.

Preparation time **30 minutes + overnight freezing**
Total cooking time **5–10 minutes**
Serves 6

175 g (5³/4 oz) caster sugar
50 g (1³/4 oz) cocoa powder
125 g (4 oz) good-quality dark chocolate, chopped

RASPBERRY COULIS
1 kg (2 lb) fresh raspberries
2 tablespoons icing sugar
few drops of lemon juice

1 Put 500 ml (16 fl oz) water with the sugar in a medium saucepan. Heat gently, stirring to dissolve the sugar, then bring to the boil. Remove the pan from the heat and add the cocoa powder and chocolate. Whisk to melt the chocolate and blend smoothly.
2 Return the pan to the heat and bring to the boil. As bubbles just break across the surface, immediately remove from the heat, place the pan in a bowl of iced water and leave for at least 10 minutes, or until thoroughly cooled. Pour the mixture into an ice cream machine and churn for 20 minutes, or until set. Pour into a 1 litre container and freeze overnight. Alternatively, pour the mixture into a 1 litre container and freeze for 3 hours, or until firm. Scoop into a large bowl and beat with electric beaters for 1–2 minutes, or until thick and smooth. Return to container, freeze for 3 hours and repeat beating and freezing twice more before pouring into the container to freeze overnight.
3 To make the raspberry coulis, place the raspberries, sugar and lemon juice in a food processor, and process until smooth. Strain to remove the seeds.
4 Serve the sorbet on chilled plates with the coulis.

Yule log

The shape of this traditional French Christmas cake is inspired by the yule log that burns on the hearth on Christmas Eve. The yule log fire is said to represent the triumph of light over darkness.

Preparation time **45 minutes + refrigeration**
Total cooking time **25 minutes**
Serves 8–12

CHOCOLATE SPONGE
2 eggs
3 tablespoons caster sugar
4 tablespoons plain flour
2 teaspoons cocoa powder

BUTTER CREAM
30 g (1 oz) bittersweet chocolate, chopped
100 g (3 1/4 oz) caster sugar
2 egg yolks
225 g (7 1/4 oz) unsalted butter, softened

GANACHE
250 g (8 oz) bittersweet chocolate, chopped
150 ml (5 fl oz) thick (double) cream
30 g (1 oz) unsalted butter

ready-made marzipan and colouring, to decorate

1 To make the chocolate sponge, preheat the oven to moderately hot 200°C (400°F/Gas 6). Line a 23 x 30 cm (9 x 12 inch) swiss roll tin with baking paper. Put the eggs and sugar in a large bowl. Half fill a saucepan with water and bring to the boil. Remove from the heat and place the bowl over the pan, making sure it is not touching the water. Using electric beaters, whisk for 5–7 minutes, or until the mixture is thick and creamy, has doubled in volume and leaves a trail as it falls from the beaters. The mixture should never be hot, only warm. Remove the bowl from the pan and whisk until cold. Sift the flour and cocoa and carefully fold into the egg mixture until just combined. Pour into the tin and spread evenly. Bake for 6–8 minutes, or until springy. Slide the hot sponge, with the paper, onto a wire rack.

2 To make the butter cream, put the chocolate in a bowl. Half fill a saucepan with water and bring to the boil. Remove from the heat and place the bowl over the pan, making sure it is not touching the water. Leave the chocolate to melt slowly, then remove from the pan. Put the sugar in a small pan with enough cold water to just cover it. Make a sugar syrup by following the method in the Chef's techniques on page 62. Meanwhile, whisk the egg yolks in a small bowl with electric beaters until pale. As soon as the syrup is ready, carefully pour the bubbling sugar in a thin steady stream onto the egg yolks, whisking continuously and pouring between the beaters and the side of the bowl. Continue whisking until cold. Whisk in the butter and then the chocolate. Place in a clean bowl and cover with plastic wrap.

3 To make the ganache, melt the chocolate as in step 2. Heat the cream until just at boiling point. Pour onto the chocolate and whisk until thick and glossy. Stir in the butter until melted, then cool to room temperature.

4 Turn the sponge over onto a large piece of greaseproof paper and peel off the paper that was used for baking. Spread the ganache over the sponge and roll it up by picking up the paper at one of the long ends and pushing it away from you while rolling. Trim the ends and chill for 5–10 minutes. Put the butter cream in a piping bag fitted with a 1 cm (1/2 inch) star nozzle. Pipe lines of butter cream lengthways along the log, then pipe swirls of butter cream on top. Alternatively, spread the butter cream with a palette knife. Chill, then use a fork to mark lines and notches for a bark effect.

5 Decorate with marzipan holly leaves and berries. Colour the marzipan with food colouring, and cut out green leaves and roll red berries between your fingers.

Hot chocolate soufflés

A well-risen, feather-light soufflé is one of the hallmarks of a great chef. The real difficulty lies in transporting the soufflé to the table before it begins to cool and collapses.

*Preparation time **20 minutes***
*Total cooking time **20–25 minutes***
*Serves **6***

50 g (1³/4 oz) good-quality dark chocolate, roughly chopped
250 ml (8 fl oz) milk
60 g (2 oz) unsalted butter
3 tablespoons plain flour
caster sugar, to coat dishes
4 eggs, separated
2¹/₂ tablespoons caster sugar
1 tablespoon cocoa powder, sifted
icing sugar, to dust

1 Preheat the oven to moderate 180°C (350°F/Gas 4). Put the chocolate in a bowl. Heat the milk in a saucepan until just at boiling point. Pour onto the chocolate and stir until the chocolate has melted. Melt the butter in a saucepan and add the flour. Cook over low heat for 1 minute. Add the chocolate milk gradually, stirring continuously with a wooden spoon. Bring to the boil and remove from the heat. Set aside to cool completely.

2 Brush six 10 x 5 cm (4 x 2 inch), 250 ml (8 fl oz) soufflé dishes with butter, working the brush from the bottom upwards. Refrigerate until the butter is firm, then repeat. Half fill one of the dishes with caster sugar and, without placing your fingers inside the mould, rotate so that a layer of sugar sticks to the butter. Tap out the excess sugar and use to coat the other moulds.

3 Stir the yolks into the chocolate mixture. In a separate bowl, whisk the egg whites with electric beaters until soft peaks form. Add the sugar and whisk for 30 seconds. Fold in the cocoa powder. Lightly beat a third of the egg-white mixture into the chocolate mixture to just blend. Add the rest of the egg-white mixture and fold in very gently but quickly. Do not overmix or the mixture will lose its volume.

4 Spoon in the mixture to fill each dish completely and level the top with a palette knife. Sprinkle with sifted icing sugar and then run your thumb just inside the top of the dish to create a ridge, which will enable the soufflé mixture to rise evenly. Bake for 15 minutes, or until the soufflés are well risen and a light crust has formed. The soufflés should feel just set when pressed lightly with your fingers. Dust the tops lightly with sifted icing sugar and serve immediately.

Chocolate rum truffles

In the true style of truffles, these petits fours are highly decadent and very rich.
They are delicious served with coffee as a special after-dinner treat.

Preparation time **40 minutes + refrigeration**
Total cooking time **10 minutes**
Makes 24

300 g (10 oz) good-quality dark chocolate,
  finely chopped
100 ml (3¼ fl oz) thick (double) cream
1 teaspoon vanilla extract or essence
25 ml (¾ fl oz) dark rum
cocoa powder, to dust

1 Put the chopped chocolate in a bowl. Place the cream and vanilla in a small saucepan and heat until it is just at boiling point. Pour the cream directly over the chopped chocolate. Gently mix with a whisk until the mixture is smooth. If there are any lumps, place the bowl over a pan of barely steaming water, off the heat, and lightly stir for a moment to melt any remaining chocolate. Mix in the rum and refrigerate the ganache until it is set.

2 Form the ganache into small balls using a melon baller, or pipe it into small balls using a piping bag fitted with a plain nozzle. Return to the refrigerator to set. Roll the balls between your palms to form a perfect ball, then roll in the cocoa powder, using a fork to roll them around until evenly coated.

Chef's tip Since these truffles are not dipped in chocolate before they are rolled in the cocoa powder, they should be eaten within 2–3 days. Store in an airtight container in the refrigerator. Roll the truffles in the cocoa powder a second time before serving.

Chocolate roulade

Whipped cream and fresh raspberries fill this delicate chocolate sponge. It is also delicious with other fresh fruits, such as strawberries or peaches.

*Preparation time **25 minutes + 20 minutes refrigeration***
*Total cooking time **8–10 minutes***
Serves 6

CHOCOLATE SPONGE
2 eggs
3 tablespoons caster sugar
4 tablespoons plain flour
2 teaspoons cocoa powder

FILLING
150 ml (5 fl oz) cream, for whipping
2¹/₂ tablespoons icing sugar
200 g (6¹/₂ oz) fresh raspberries

cocoa powder and icing sugar, to dust

1 To make the sponge, preheat the oven to moderately hot 200°C (400°F/Gas 6). Line a 23 x 30 cm (9 x 12 inch) swiss roll tin with baking paper. Put the eggs and sugar in a large bowl. Half fill a saucepan with water and bring to the boil. Remove from the heat and place the bowl over the saucepan, making sure it is not touching the water. The water should be steaming.

Using electric beaters, whisk for 5–7 minutes, or until the mixture becomes thick and creamy, has doubled in volume and leaves a trail as it falls from the beaters. The temperature of the mixture should never be hot, only warm. Remove the bowl from the water and continue to whisk until the mixture is cold.

2 Sift the flour and cocoa powder together and, using a large metal spoon, carefully fold into the whisked mixture. Stop folding as soon as the flour and cocoa powder are just combined or the mixture will lose its volume. Pour the mixture into the tin and spread it evenly using a palette knife. Bake for 6–8 minutes, or until springy to the light touch of a finger. Remove the sponge from the tin while still hot by sliding it, with the paper on, to a wire rack to cool. Leave to cool, then turn over onto a large piece of greaseproof paper or clean cloth and remove the paper that was used for baking.

3 To make the filling, whip the cream with the icing sugar until firm peaks form. Spread the cream onto the chocolate sponge and sprinkle with the raspberries. Roll up by picking up the paper or cloth at one of the longer ends and pushing it down and away from you while rolling, finishing with the seam underneath. Trim each end and refrigerate for 20 minutes. Sprinkle a little sifted cocoa powder and icing sugar onto the roulade.

Warm chocolate desserts with pistachio cream

*These little chocolate puddings, served with a sweet pistachio cream and
poached pears, are an ideal winter dessert.*

Preparation time **20 minutes**
Total cooking time **35 minutes**
Serves 8

PISTACHIO CREAM
20 g (³/4 oz) pistachio nuts, chopped
250 ml (8 fl oz) milk
3 egg yolks
2¹/2 tablespoons caster sugar
1–2 drops vanilla extract or essence

185 g (6 oz) good-quality dark chocolate, chopped
150 g (5 oz) unsalted butter, softened
3¹/2 tablespoons cocoa powder, sifted
6 eggs, separated
225 g (7¹/4 oz) caster sugar
poached or canned pears, drained and sliced, to serve

1 To make the pistachio cream, toast the pistachios
under a grill for 1–2 minutes, shaking to make sure they
don't burn. Grind the nuts to a paste using a mortar and
pestle or a food processor. Pour the milk into a saucepan
and heat slowly until just at boiling point. Meanwhile,
cream together the egg yolks and sugar until pale. Pour
the milk onto the yolks, mixing well. Transfer to a clean
pan and cook gently over low heat, stirring constantly,
until the mixture begins to thicken and coats the back
of a spoon. Remove from the heat immediately, strain
into a bowl and stir in the vanilla extract or essence, to
taste. Whisk in the pistachio paste and chill.
2 Preheat the oven to warm 160°C (315°F/Gas 2–3).
Brush eight 8 x 3.5 cm (3 x 1¹/4 inch), 150 ml (5 fl oz)
ramekins with melted butter. Put the chocolate in a
bowl. Half fill a saucepan with water and bring to the
boil. Remove from the heat and place the bowl over the
pan, making sure it is not touching the water. Leave the
chocolate to melt slowly. Cream the butter until soft
with a wooden spoon. Stir in the cocoa powder and fold
in the chocolate.
3 In a separate bowl, whisk the egg yolks and 125 g
(4 oz) of the sugar until doubled in volume, then fold
into the chocolate mixture. Whisk the egg whites until
stiff peaks form. Add the remaining sugar and whisk to
a stiff, shiny meringue. Fold carefully into the chocolate
mixture in three additions until just combined. Spoon
into the ramekins to three-quarters full. Bake for about
25 minutes, or until set, then remove from the ramekins
and place on individual plates. Pour the chilled pistachio
cream around and serve immediately with the pears.

Opéra

Adapted from a complex French recipe, this dessert is a true work of art. It consists of layers of sponge cake, chocolate ganache, butter cream and coffee syrup, finished with a rich chocolate topping.

Preparation time **1 hour 45 minutes + refrigeration**
Total cooking time **1 hour**
Serves **4–6**

ALMOND SPONGE
75 g (2¹/₂ oz) icing sugar
2¹/₂ tablespoons plain flour
75 g (2¹/₂ oz) ground almonds
3 eggs
15 g (¹/₂ oz) unsalted butter, melted and cooled
3 egg whites
1 tablespoon caster sugar

CHOCOLATE GANACHE
200 g (6¹/₂ oz) good-quality dark chocolate, finely chopped
120 ml (4 fl oz) milk
110 ml (3³/₄ fl oz) thick (double) cream
50 g (1³/₄ oz) unsalted butter, softened

COFFEE SYRUP
1¹/₂ tablespoons caster sugar
1¹/₂ tablespoons instant coffee

BUTTER CREAM
70 g (2¹/₄ oz) caster sugar
1 egg white
1 tablespoon instant coffee
100 g (3¹/₄ oz) unsalted butter, softened

1 To make the sponge, preheat the oven to hot 220°C (425°F/Gas 7). Line a 20 x 30 cm (8 x 12 inch) baking tin with baking paper. Sift the icing sugar and flour into a large bowl. Stir in the almonds. Add the eggs and whisk until pale. Fold in the butter. Whisk the egg whites until stiff, add the sugar and whisk until stiff peaks form. Whisk a third of the egg-white mixture into the almond mixture, then carefully fold in the remaining egg-white mixture until just combined. Pour onto the tray and gently spread. Bake for 6–7 minutes, or until golden and springy. Loosen the edges with the point of a knife. Turn out onto a wire rack covered with baking paper. Do not remove the paper used in baking.

2 To make the ganache, put the chocolate in a bowl. Heat the milk and 30 ml (1 fl oz) of the cream until just at boiling point. Pour onto the chocolate, add the butter and mix until smooth. Allow to set until spreadable.

3 To make the coffee syrup, put the sugar and 90 ml (3 fl oz) water in a pan and stir until dissolved. Bring to the boil and add the coffee.

4 To make the butter cream, put the sugar and 3 teaspoons of water in a small heavy-based pan. Make a sugar syrup by following the method in the Chef's techniques on page 62. Meanwhile, whisk the egg white until very soft peaks form. Continue whisking and carefully pour in the hot syrup, pouring between the beaters and the side of the bowl. Whisk until cold. Dissolve the coffee in 1 teaspoon of boiling water, cool to room temperature and add to the butter. Beat in half the egg-white mixture, then carefully fold in the other half until well combined.

5 Cut the sponge into three pieces, each 10 x 20 cm (4 x 8 inches). Soak one piece with a third of the coffee syrup, then spread with half the butter cream. Cover with the second piece of sponge, soak with syrup and spread with half the ganache. Cover with the last piece of sponge, soak with the remaining syrup and top with the remaining butter cream. Smooth the top and refrigerate until the butter cream is firmly set.

6 Melt the remaining ganache over a pan of simmering water. Heat the remaining cream until just at boiling point and stir into the ganache. Cool until spreadable and spread over the top of the cake.

Chocolate tart

*With a creamy chocolate centre and pastry that melts in your mouth, this tart is delicious accompanied
by a whisky-flavoured ice cream or a spoonful of vanilla-flavoured crème fraîche.*

Preparation time **50 minutes**
   + 1 hour 40 minutes refrigeration
Total cooking time **30–35 minutes**
Serves 8

PASTRY
125 g (4 oz) unsalted butter, softened
2¹/₂ tablespoons caster sugar
I egg, beaten
I–2 drops vanilla extract or essence
200 g (6¹/₂ oz) plain flour, sifted
pinch of salt

250 g (8 oz) bittersweet chocolate, chopped
2 eggs
4 egg yolks
3 tablespoons caster sugar
**200 g (6¹/₂ oz) softened unsalted butter, cut into
   cubes**
icing sugar, to dust

1 To make the pastry, cream the butter and sugar
together with a wooden spoon. Gradually beat in the
combined egg and vanilla, beating well after each
addition. (The mixture may look slightly curdled.) Add
the flour and salt, and mix lightly until smooth. Do not
overmix. Gather the pastry together into a rough ball.
Flatten with the palm of your hand to a thickness of
1 cm (¹/₂ inch), wrap in plastic wrap and refrigerate for
20 minutes.
2 Grease a 24 x 2.5 cm (9¹/₂ x 1 inch) loose-bottomed
fluted flan tin. Preheat the oven to moderate 180°C
(350°F/Gas 4).

3 Roll the pastry out on a floured surface to a circle
about 3 mm (¹/₈ inch) thick. Fold half the pastry over
the rolling pin and lift into the tin. Ease the sides of the
pastry into the flutes or sides of the tin by using a small
ball of lightly floured excess pastry held between your
forefinger and thumb. Trim off any excess pastry with a
sharp knife or roll over the top of the tin with a rolling
pin. Chill for 20 minutes. Cut a 27 cm (10³/₄ inch)
circle of greaseproof paper, crush it into a ball to soften
the paper, then open and lay inside the pastry so that it
comes up the sides. Fill with baking beans up to the rim,
then press down gently, so the beans rest firmly against
the sides of the flan. Bake for 10 minutes, or until firm.
Remove and discard the paper and beans. Return to the
oven and continue to bake for 5–10 minutes, or until the
centre begins to colour. Remove from the oven and
allow to cool.
4 Put the chocolate in a bowl. Half fill a saucepan with
water and bring to the boil. Remove from the heat and
place the bowl over the pan, making sure it is not
touching the water. Leave the chocolate to melt slowly,
then remove the bowl from the pan. Meanwhile, place
the eggs, egg yolks and sugar in a bowl over a pan of
barely steaming water and whisk until well combined,
pale and four times its original volume.
5 Stir one piece of butter at a time into the chocolate.
Gently fold in the egg mixture until thoroughly
combined, but do not overmix or it will lose its volume.
Pour into the pastry and bake for 10 minutes. Cool
slightly before removing from the tin. Cool, then chill
for 1 hour before serving. Dust with icing sugar.

Chef's tip Any leftover pastry may be frozen in an
airtight container for later use.

Orange-flavoured chocolate-dipped cookies

The word cookie originates from the Dutch 'koekje', which means 'little cakes. These 'little cakes' are dipped in dark chocolate for an elegant touch.

Preparation time **15 minutes + refrigeration**
Total cooking time **7–8 minutes**
Makes 18

100 g (3¼ oz) unsalted butter, at room temperature
2½ tablespoons caster sugar
finely grated rind of ½ orange
125 g (4 oz) self-raising flour
100 g (3¼ oz) good-quality dark chocolate, chopped

1 Preheat the oven to moderately hot 190°C (375°F/ Gas 5). Brush a baking tray with melted butter. Soften the butter with a wooden spoon, gradually add the sugar and orange rind, and beat until pale. Sift the flour and stir in until just combined. Roll the mixture into balls the size of a walnut. Place on the tray and flatten with a wet fork. Bake for 7–8 minutes, or until golden brown. Cool on a wire rack.
2 Meanwhile, put the chocolate in a bowl. Half fill a saucepan with water and bring to the boil. Remove from the heat and place the bowl over the pan, making sure it is not touching the water. Leave the chocolate to melt slowly, then remove the bowl from the pan. Dip one side of each biscuit into the chocolate and lay on greaseproof paper. Refrigerate the biscuits until the chocolate is just set.

Chef's tip These biscuits may be stored in an airtight container for up to a week.

Irish coffee cream

If you simply can't wait for the ganache to go cold before you indulge in this treat, try serving it warm.

Preparation time **10 minutes + refrigeration**
Total cooking time **3–5 minutes**
Serves 4

GANACHE
200 g (6½ oz) dark bittersweet chocolate, chopped
200 ml (6½ fl oz) thick (double) cream
2 tablespoons caster sugar
I tablespoon whisky

COFFEE CREAM
200 ml (6½ fl oz) cream, for whipping
3 tablespoons icing sugar, sifted
I tablespoon coffee extract (see Chef's tip)

cocoa powder, to dust

1 To make the ganache, put the chocolate in a bowl. Put the cream and sugar in a saucepan and heat until just at boiling point. Pour directly onto the chocolate and mix well until smooth and creamy. (If the chocolate does not melt, stir over a pan of hot water, making sure the bowl is not touching the water.) Mix in the whisky. Refrigerate to cool, mixing from time to time to prevent a crust forming on the surface.
2 Divide the ganache among four glasses or goblets, and chill while preparing the coffee cream.
3 To make the coffee cream, whip the cream and sugar until firm peaks form. Mix in the coffee extract. Pipe the coffee cream onto the ganache, then lightly dust with cocoa powder before serving.

Chef's tip If coffee extract is difficult to find, use 1 tablespoon of instant coffee granules dissolved in 1 teaspoon of hot water.

Orange-flavoured chocolate-dipped cookies (bottom) and Irish coffee cream

Chocolate beignets

These little fritters are crisp on the outside, with a soft, chocolaty filling.
They are delicious served hot with vanilla ice cream.

Preparation time **1 hour 20 minutes + chilling**
Total cooking time **30 minutes**
Makes 48

300 g (10 oz) good-quality dark chocolate, chopped
200 ml (6¹/2 fl oz) thick (double) cream
cocoa powder, to dust
oil, for deep-frying
flour, to dust

BEIGNET BATTER
250 g (8 oz) plain flour
1 tablespoon potato flour or cornflour
1 tablespoon oil
pinch of salt
1 egg
225 ml (7¹/4 fl oz) beer
2 egg whites
1 tablespoon caster sugar

1 Put the chopped chocolate in a bowl. Half fill a saucepan with water and bring to the boil. Remove from the heat and place the bowl over the pan, making sure it is not touching the water. Leave the chocolate to melt slowly, then remove the bowl from the pan. Heat the cream in a small saucepan until it is just at boiling point. Pour onto the chocolate and whisk until smooth. Scrape down the sides of the bowl, cover and chill until set.

2 Once the chocolate has set, scoop it into a pastry bag and pipe out 48 small balls onto baking paper—don't worry if they are not perfectly round. Refrigerate until hardened, then roll between your hands to form uniform balls, using cocoa powder to prevent them from sticking too much. Freeze until solid.

3 To make the batter, mix the flour and potato flour together in a large bowl, and make a well in the centre. Add the oil, salt and egg, and mix together, gradually incorporating the flour. Once a smooth paste has formed, mix in the beer, a little at a time. Continue working until the batter is smooth.

4 Pour the oil into a deep-fryer and preheat it to 200°C (400°F), or one-third fill a large heavy-based saucepan with oil and preheat it to moderately hot. Beat the egg whites until firm, then beat in the sugar and gently fold into the batter. Remove two or three balls at a time from the freezer and lightly coat with some flour. Using tongs, dip the balls into the batter and place directly into the hot oil. Fry for 3–5 minutes, or until lightly browned. Do not fry too many at a time or the temperature of the oil will drop. Remove immediately and drain on paper towels. Continue with the remaining balls. Lightly dust with cocoa powder before serving.

Chef's tip It is very important that the chocolate is completely frozen before deep-frying. If you have time, prepare the chocolate balls the day before and freeze them overnight.

Creamy chocolate soufflés

This soufflé has a creamier texture than a conventional soufflé, so it won't
rise as much. It is best made in individual shallow dishes.

Preparation time **10 minutes**
Total cooking time **15 minutes**
Serves 4

100 g (3¹/4 oz) good-quality dark chocolate, chopped
60 g (2 oz) unsalted butter
3 tablespoons cocoa powder
2 eggs, separated
caster sugar, to coat dishes
2 egg whites
50 g (1³/4 oz) icing sugar, sifted, plus extra to dust
vanilla ice cream or orange sorbet, to serve

1 Preheat the oven to moderately hot 200°C (400°F/ Gas 6). Put the chocolate in a bowl. Half fill a saucepan with water and bring to the boil. Remove from the heat and place the bowl over the pan, making sure it is not touching the water. Leave the chocolate to melt slowly, then add the butter and whisk until smooth. Sift the cocoa onto the melted chocolate and mix well. Remove the bowl from the pan. Whisk the egg yolks and then add to the chocolate mixture.

2 Lightly butter four 12.5 x 2.5 cm (5 x 1 inch), 300 ml (10 fl oz) gratin dishes. Coat lightly with some of the sugar and set aside. Whisk the egg whites in a large bowl until stiff peaks form. Gradually whisk in the icing sugar and whisk until the whites are firm and shiny. Gently fold a third of the egg-white mixture into the chocolate mixture. Once incorporated, fold in the remaining egg-white mixture. Divide the mixture among the dishes. Sprinkle with icing sugar and bake for about 8 minutes, or until the soufflés are just set to the light touch of a finger. Place a scoop of ice cream or sorbet in the centre and serve immediately.

Chef's tip Eggs are easiest to separate when they are cold, straight from the refrigerator. However, to get maximum volume from egg whites, they are best beaten at room temperature. Egg whites should be beaten in a clean dry bowl with clean, dry beaters. Any hint of grease will prevent them aerating.

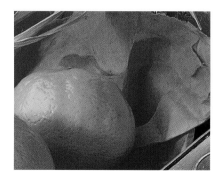

Chocolate-dipped fruits

Surely this is the way fruit was intended to be...sweet and juicy, and smothered with rich dark chocolate. The combination of fruits you use is only limited by your imagination.

Preparation time **20 minutes + 15 minutes refrigeration**
Total cooking time **10–15 minutes**
Serves 4–6

540 g (1 lb 1 1/4 oz) strawberries
2 clementines or mandarin oranges
185 g (6 oz) bittersweet chocolate, chopped
1 tablespoon white vegetable shortening or cooking oil

1 Line a baking tray with greaseproof or baking paper. Clean the strawberries by brushing with a dry pastry brush, or rinsing them very quickly in cold water and drying well on a thick layer of paper towels. Discard any berries with soft spots. Peel the clementines or mandarin oranges and remove as much of the white pith as possible, then break the fruit into individual segments.

2 Put the chocolate in a bowl. Half fill a saucepan with water and bring to the boil. Remove from the heat and place the bowl over the pan, making sure it is not touching the water. Leave the chocolate to melt slowly. Stir in the shortening or oil, and mix until melted and completely incorporated. Remove the bowl from the pan and place on a folded towel to keep it warm.

3 Holding the berries by their stems or hulls, dip about three quarters of the way into the chocolate, so that some of the colour of the fruit still shows. Gently wipe off any excess chocolate on the edge of the bowl and place the coated strawberries on their sides on the tray. Repeat with the clementines or mandarins, drying each segment on paper towels before dipping. If the chocolate becomes too thick, reheat the water, remove from the heat and place the bowl over the pan until the chocolate returns to the required consistency.

4 Once all the fruit has been dipped in the chocolate, place in the refrigerator for 15 minutes, or until the chocolate has just set. Remove from the refrigerator and keep in a cool place until ready to serve. Do not serve directly from the refrigerator—the cold temperature will inhibit the full flavour and sweetness of the fruit, and the chocolate will be too hard.

Chef's tips Any fruit can be used, but the best results are with ones that can be left whole or have a dry surface.

If the strawberry stems are too short, use a toothpick to dip them.

Use a small pair of tongs for the clementine or mandarin slices—do not use a toothpick as it will pierce the fruit, and the juices will prevent the chocolate from coating evenly.

Truffle torte

This is a truly decadent, rich chocolate dessert. Serve it just as it is with a strong espresso or with a bowl of fresh raspberries. Either way, this smooth, rich torte is enough to impress anyone.

Preparation time **1 hour 30 minutes + refrigeration**
Total cooking time **20 minutes**
Serves 8

CHOCOLATE SPONGE
2 eggs
2¹/₂ tablespoons caster sugar
4 tablespoons plain flour
1 tablespoon cocoa powder

30 ml (1 fl oz) rum
535 g (1 lb 1¹/₄ oz) good-quality dark chocolate, chopped
2 gelatine leaves or 1 teaspoon gelatine powder
65 g (2¹/₄ oz) liquid glucose
500 ml (16 fl oz) cream, for whipping
cocoa powder, to dust

1 To make the sponge, preheat the oven to warm 170°C (325°F/Gas 3). Butter and flour a 20 x 5.5 cm (8 x 2¹/₄ inch) round springform tin. Half fill a saucepan with water, bring to the boil and remove from the heat. Put the eggs and sugar in a large bowl and place over the saucepan, making sure it is not touching the water. Using electric beaters, whisk for 5–10 minutes, or until the mixture is thick and light, has doubled in volume and leaves a trail as it falls from the whisk. The temperature of the mixture should never be hot, only warm. Remove the bowl from the pan of water and continue to whisk until cold. Sift the flour and cocoa powder together and carefully fold into the whisked mixture with a large metal spoon or plastic spatula, until just combined. Pour the mixture into the tin, gently smooth the top with the back of a spoon and bake for about 15 minutes, or until springy and shrinking from the side of the tin. Turn out onto a wire

rack to cool. Clean the cake tin ready to use later.

2 Trim the top crust from the sponge using a long serrated knife. Cut the cake into a disc no more than 1.5 cm (5/8 inch) thick to just fit inside the tin and place on a 20 cm (8 inch) cake card inside the tin or directly on the base of the tin. Brush the sponge disc with rum.

3 Put 335 g (10³/4 oz) of the chocolate in a bowl. Half fill a saucepan with water and bring to the boil. Remove from the heat and place the bowl over the pan, making sure it is not touching the water. Leave the chocolate to melt slowly, then remove the bowl from the pan. Soften the gelatine leaves in cold water or stir the gelatine powder and 1 tablespoon water over a pan of simmering water until dissolved. Pour 100 ml (3¹/4 fl oz) water into a small pan, add the glucose and bring to the boil. Remove from the heat. Drain the gelatine leaves by squeezing them tightly in your hand, then stir the gelatine leaves or dissolved gelatine powder into the warm glucose syrup until completely dissolved. Pour onto the chocolate, mixing thoroughly with a small wire whisk. If this mixture is lumpy, heat very gently over a pan of barely steaming water off the heat until the mixture is smooth. Leave to cool.

4 Whip the cream until soft peaks form, and fold it into the cooled chocolate mixture. Do not overmix. Fill the tin to the top with the truffle mixture and level with a palette knife. Refrigerate for several hours, or until set.

5 Hold a hot, damp towel around the tin for 30 seconds and lift out the torte. Dust the torte with the cocoa powder and mark it with the back of a knife in a trellis fashion. Melt the remaining chocolate in a bowl over hot water as before. Pour onto a sheet of non-stick baking paper and spread to a thickness of 2 mm (1/8 inch) with a large palette knife. Refrigerate until set. Break off large pieces of chocolate from the paper and stick on the side of the torte. Transfer the torte, on the card or tin base, to a large plate, to serve.

Petits pots au chocolat

These dainty little chocolate custards are prepared and cooked in a very similar way to crème caramel, except that they are much richer, with a fine, smooth texture that melts in the mouth.

Preparation time **10 minutes + refrigeration**
Total cooking time **45 minutes**
Serves 6

375 ml (12 fl oz) milk
150 ml (5 fl oz) cream
50 g (1³/4 oz) good-quality dark chocolate, chopped
¹/2 vanilla pod, split lengthways
1 egg
3 egg yolks
100 g (3¹/4 oz) caster sugar
whipped cream and grated chocolate, to serve

1 Preheat the oven to warm 170°C (325°F/Gas 3). Place the milk, cream, chocolate and vanilla pod in a heavy-based pan and bring to the boil. Using a wooden spoon, cream the egg, egg yolks and sugar together until thick and light. Pour in the melted chocolate mixture and stir to blend. Strain into a jug and discard the vanilla pod. Remove any froth by skimming across the top with a metal spoon.

2 Pour the mixture into six 100 ml (3¹/4 fl oz) ramekins, filling them up to the top. Set the ramekins in a baking dish and pour in enough hot water to come up to about 1 cm (¹/2 inch) below their rims. Bake for 30 minutes, or until the surface of the custard feels elastic when you touch it with your finger, and your finger comes away clean. If this is not the case, continue to cook for a little while longer. Remove the ramekins from the water bath and allow to cool. Once cold, place the whipped cream in a piping bag fitted with a star-shaped nozzle. Pipe rosettes of cream onto the top of the ramekins and sprinkle with a little grated chocolate.

Symphony of three chocolates

The harmonious composition of the layers of creamy white, milk and dark chocolate mousse will be sweet music to your mouth.

*Preparation time **1 hour + 3 hours refrigeration***
*Total cooking time **20 minutes***
Serves 8–10

ITALIAN MERINGUE
200 g (6½ oz) caster sugar
6 egg whites

WHITE CHOCOLATE MOUSSE
1 gelatine leaf or ½ teaspoon gelatine powder
70 g (2¼ oz) good-quality white chocolate, chopped
30 ml (1 fl oz) Cointreau
60 ml (2 fl oz) cream, whipped
juice of ¼ lemon

MILK CHOCOLATE MOUSSE
1 gelatine leaf or ½ teaspoon gelatine powder
70 g (2¼ oz) good-quality milk chocolate, chopped
60 ml (2 fl oz) cream, whipped

DARK CHOCOLATE MOUSSE
1 gelatine leaf or ½ teaspoon gelatine powder
70 g (2¼ oz) good-quality dark chocolate, chopped
60 ml (2 fl oz) cream, whipped

1 To make the Italian meringue, put the sugar and 50 ml (1¾ fl oz) water in a small saucepan. Make a sugar syrup by following the method in the Chef's techniques on page 62. Meanwhile, whisk the egg whites with electric beaters until stiff peaks form. When the syrup is ready, immediately dip the bottom of the pan in cold water to stop the cooking process. Carefully pour the hot syrup onto the egg whites in a steady stream, whisking continuously and pouring between the beaters and the side of the bowl. Continue beating at moderate speed until the mixture is completely cool.

Cover with plastic wrap.

2 Lightly grease a 23.5 x 7.5 x 6.5 cm (9¼ x 3 x 2½ inch), 1 litre terrine pan and line the base with baking paper extending over the ends of the dish.

3 To make the white chocolate mousse, soften the gelatine leaf in cold water or stir the gelatine powder and 1 tablespoon water over a pan of simmering water until dissolved. Put the white chocolate in a bowl. Half fill a saucepan with water and bring to the boil. Remove from the heat and place the bowl over the pan, making sure it is not touching the water. Leave the chocolate to melt slowly. Once the gelatine leaf has softened, squeeze out the excess water. Place the gelatine leaf or dissolved gelatine powder in a bowl with the Cointreau and melt over a pan of hot water. Fold a third of the cream into the melted chocolate. Mix some of this into the gelatine mixture, then fold into the chocolate mixture. Fold in the remaining cream, a third of the Italian meringue and the lemon juice. Transfer to the terrine pan and spread in an even layer using the back of a spoon. Refrigerate to set.

4 To make the milk chocolate mousse, follow the same method as step 3, replacing the Cointreau with 30 ml (1 fl oz) water and omitting the lemon juice. Spread evenly over the white chocolate mousse and return to the refrigerator until set.

5 To make the dark chocolate mousse, follow the same method as step 3, replacing the Cointreau with 30 ml (1 fl oz) water and omitting the lemon juice. Spread evenly over the milk chocolate mousse. Refrigerate for at least 3 hours, or overnight.

6 Run the tip of a knife along the edge of the terrine pan. Dip the base in hot water for a few seconds, place a cutting board on top and flip over. Hold the terrine pan and cutting board securely and shake downwards. Repeat this process if necessary. Gently lift the terrine pan away. Cut into slices to serve.

White chocolate fudge

Made with creamy white chocolate, this fudge is ultra sweet, so eat it in small quantities, if you can.

Preparation time **15 minutes + 2 hours refrigeration**
Total cooking time **7 minutes**
Makes about 50 pieces

350 g (11¼ oz) caster sugar
30 g (1 oz) unsalted butter
pinch of salt
125 ml (4 fl oz) evaporated milk
1 vanilla pod
300 g (10 oz) good-quality white chocolate, chopped
80 g (2¾ oz) pistachio nuts

1 Grease an 18 cm (7 inch) square cake tin. Put the sugar, butter, salt and evaporated milk in a large saucepan. Split the vanilla pod in half lengthways and scrape the small black seeds into the saucepan with the point of a knife. Add the pod to the saucepan. Bring to the boil over medium heat, stirring continuously with a wooden spoon. Lower the heat and simmer for about 5 minutes, stirring continuously.
2 Remove the saucepan from the heat and lift out the vanilla pod with a fork or slotted spoon. Stir in the chopped chocolate until it has melted completely and the mixture is smooth. Stir in the pistachios and pour into the tin. Refrigerate for about 2 hours, or until firm.
3 Cut into small squares and serve in petit four paper cases. Store in the refrigerator for up to a week.

Chef's tips Chopped hazelnuts may be substituted for the pistachios.

Using a vanilla pod will give a delicious flavour to the fudge, but if you wish to avoid seeing the black seeds, use ½ teaspoon vanilla extract or essence instead.

Chocolate Genoese sponge

This recipe is named after the city of Genoa, where this classic sponge is thought to have been created. The secret to a successful Genoese sponge is in treating the mixture carefully. If the eggs and sugar are beaten correctly, and the flour is lightly folded through, the result should be a feather-light sponge.

Preparation time **15 minutes + cooling**
Total cooking time **35–40 minutes**
Serves 8–10

4 eggs
100 g (3¼ oz) caster sugar
80 g (2¾ oz) plain flour
2 tablespoons cocoa powder
20 g (¾ oz) unsalted butter, melted
120 g (4 oz) raspberry jam
icing sugar, to dust

1 Preheat the oven to moderate 180°C (350°F/Gas 4). Grease and lightly flour a 20 cm (8 inch) round cake tin. Put the eggs and sugar in a large bowl. Half fill a saucepan with water and heat until just steaming. Remove from the heat and place the bowl over the saucepan, making sure that the bowl is not touching the water. Using electric beaters, beat for 5–10 minutes, or until the mixture is thick and creamy, has doubled in volume and leaves a trail as it falls from the beaters. The mixture should never be hot, only warm. Remove the

bowl from the pan and continue to beat until cold.

2 Sift the flour and cocoa powder together and, using a large metal spoon, carefully fold into the whisked mixture. Stop folding as soon as the flour and cocoa powder are just combined or the mixture will lose its volume. Gently, but quickly, fold in the warm butter. Pour into the tin and bake on the middle shelf of the oven for 25–30 minutes, or until springy to the light touch of a finger and shrinking from the sides of the tin. Turn out onto a wire rack, put another rack on top, turn over so the crust is uppermost, remove the rack that is now on top and leave to cool. This ensures that the top crust is not broken or marked by the wire.

3 Using a long serrated knife, cut the cold cake in half horizontally, cutting from one side to the other with a firm sawing action. Spread the bottom half with the raspberry jam. Place the other half on top, sprinkle with icing sugar and carefully lift onto a plate.

Chef's tips The saucepan of water in step 1 must not be too hot as this would cause the mixture to lose volume and the cake to be flat and heavy once cooked.

The unfilled sponge may be frozen for 3 months.

Chocolate mousse

This sophisticated chocolate mousse is so light and creamy that it melts in the mouth. Try serving the mousse in chocolate cups, or layering with banana and rum, or amaretti biscuits and whisky.

*Preparation time **1 hour + 1 hour refrigeration***
*Total cooking time **15 minutes***
Serves 6

140 g (4¹/2 oz) good-quality dark chocolate
3 tablespoons caster sugar
2 egg whites
1¹/2 gelatine leaves or ³/4 teaspoon gelatine powder
1 tablespoon instant coffee
500 ml (16 fl oz) cream, for whipping

1 Grate 15 g (¹/2 oz) of the chocolate and set aside in a cool dry place. Put 60 ml (2 fl oz) water with the sugar in a small heavy-based pan. Make a sugar syrup by following the method in the Chef's techniques on page 62. When the sugar starts to boil, whisk the egg whites in a bowl using electric beaters until they barely hold their shape in very soft peaks. With the machine still running, carefully pour the bubbling syrup onto the whites, aiming between the bowl and the beaters. Continue to whisk until cold.

2 Soak the gelatine leaves in a bowl of cold water for a few minutes until soft, then remove and drain, or stir the gelatine powder and 1 tablespoon water over a pan of simmering water until dissolved. Dissolve the instant coffee in 1 tablespoon of boiling water in a small pan, add the gelatine leaves or dissolved gelatine powder and warm over gentle heat. Do not boil or the gelatine will be stringy. Pour onto the egg whites and stir well.

3 Roughly chop the remaining chocolate and put in a bowl. Half fill a saucepan with water and bring to the boil. Remove from the heat and place the bowl over the pan, making sure it is not touching the water. Leave the chocolate to melt slowly, then remove from the pan and fold into the egg-white mixture.

4 Whip the cream until it leaves a trail when lifted on the whisk, then fold into the chocolate mixture. Stir in the grated chocolate. Pipe the mousse into six glasses using a piping bag fitted with a 1.5 cm (5/8 inch) plain nozzle. Refrigerate for 1 hour, or until set. The mousse can be decorated with rosettes of whipped cream or chocolate leaves, grated chocolate or chocolate curls (see Chef's techniques, page 63).

Hazelnut chocolate truffles

These divine milk-chocolate petits fours are made with hazelnut spread and a touch of Cointreau.
Rolled in icing sugar, they're the perfect size to just pop in your mouth.

*Preparation time **1 hour + refrigeration***
*Total cooking time **15 minutes***
Makes 40

600 g (1 1/4 lb) good-quality milk chocolate, chopped
30 g (1 oz) chocolate hazelnut spread
30 ml (1 fl oz) Cointreau
20 g (3/4 oz) unsalted butter
200 g (6 1/2 oz) icing sugar

1 Line a baking tray with baking paper. Put 200 g (6 1/2 oz) of the chocolate in a bowl. Half fill a saucepan with water and bring to the boil. Remove from the heat and place the bowl over the pan, making sure it is not touching the water. Leave the chocolate to melt slowly, then remove the bowl from the pan.

2 Place 30 ml (1 fl oz) water with the hazelnut spread and Cointreau in a small pan, and bring to the boil. Pour onto the melted chocolate and beat well with a wooden spoon. Stir in the butter, allow to cool, then refrigerate and allow the mixture to set. It should be stiff enough to hold its own shape when piped.

3 Spoon the mixture into a piping bag fitted with a 12 mm (1/2 inch) star-shaped nozzle, and pipe in long, straight, even lines onto the paper-lined tray. Put the tray in the refrigerator so the chocolate becomes firm.

4 Meanwhile, temper the remaining chocolate by following the method in the Chef's techniques on page 62. Place the tempered chocolate over a bowl of lukewarm water to prevent it from setting.

5 Cut the strips of piped chocolate into 2.5 cm (1 inch) lengths to fit into petit four cases. Put the icing sugar in a bowl. Using a fork, dip each truffle into the chocolate, one at a time, and shake off the excess by tapping the fork on the side of the bowl. Drop into the icing sugar and shake gently to fully coat. Allow to set in the icing sugar for a few minutes. Remove each truffle, shaking off any excess sugar, and place in a petit four case. Store in an airtight container at room temperature.

Chocolate sauce

This is the ultimate topping for ice cream, but you'll find an excuse to serve it on almost anything.

Preparation time **10 minutes**
Total cooking time **15 minutes**
Serves 4–6

225 g (7¹/4 oz) caster sugar
100 g (3¹/4 oz) good-quality dark chocolate, chopped
2 tablespoons cocoa powder, sifted

1 Put 300 ml (10 fl oz) water with the sugar and chocolate in a saucepan. Bring to the boil slowly, stirring continuously to dissolve the sugar and melt the chocolate, then remove from the heat.

2 Mix the cocoa powder with 30 ml (1 fl oz) water to form a smooth paste. Spoon into the saucepan, stir and return to medium heat. Bring back to the boil, whisking vigorously. Simmer, uncovered, for 5 minutes without allowing the sauce to boil. Strain through a fine sieve and leave to cool a little.

Chef's tip This sauce may be served hot or cold and keeps well for up to 1 week if stored in an airtight container in the refrigerator.

Hot chocolate drink

If you've only ever experienced hot chocolate made with hot milk and cocoa, you'll die for this chocolate drink made with melted chocolate, milk and cream.

Preparation time **10 minutes**
Total cooking time **15 minutes**
Makes about 1.4 litres

1 litre milk
250 ml (8 fl oz) thick (double) cream
120 g (4 oz) good-quality dark chocolate, roughly chopped
1 teaspoon ground cinnamon
1 black peppercorn
3 tablespoons caster sugar

1 Pour the milk and cream into a saucepan and slowly bring to the boil over low heat. Add the chocolate, cinnamon, peppercorn and sugar, and gently simmer for at least 10 minutes.

2 The chocolate may be strained and served immediately, but the flavour will improve if it is refrigerated for a few hours or up to 3 days. Reheat through to serve.

Chocolate sauce (bottom) and Hot chocolate drink

Chef's techniques

◆

Tempering chocolate

Tempering chocolate breaks down the fat, resulting in a hard, glossy chocolate.

Place the chopped chocolate in a heatproof bowl and sit it over a pan of water that has just boiled. Leave the chocolate to melt slowly off the heat. The bowl must not touch the water at any time.

Stir the chocolate until it is smooth and reaches a temperature of 45°C (113°F).

Sit the bowl of melted chocolate over a large bowl filled with ice cubes. Stir until the temperature drops to 25°C (77°F).

Heat the chocolate again over the pan of hot water for 30–60 seconds, or until it reaches 32°C (90°F).

Making a sugar syrup

Wait until the sugar has completely dissolved before boiling the liquid, and never stir once the syrup boils.

Stir the sugar and water over low heat until the sugar dissolves completely.

Using a wet pastry brush, brush the sugar crystals from the side of the pan.

Boil, without stirring, until the syrup reaches the soft-ball stage, which is between 116°C (241°F) and 118°C (244°F).

If you don't have a sugar thermometer, drop about 1/4 teaspoon of the syrup into a bowl of iced water. The ball of syrup should hold its shape but be soft when pressed.

Making chocolate cups

Ice cream, sorbet and mousse all look lovely served in elegant chocolate cups.

Line the inside of brioche or other moulds with plastic wrap, then fill with water. Place the moulds in the freezer until frozen solid.

Melt the chocolate. Remove the ice from the moulds, grasping the plastic wrap at the top, and immediately dip the ice mould into the melted chocolate.

Lift the ice mould from the chocolate and allow the excess to drain away. The chocolate should set immediately. Carefully peel away the plastic and discard the ice.

Making chocolate leaves

Use unsprayed leaves and make sure you wipe over them with a damp towel, then allow to dry.

Using a fine brush, paint one side of rose, ivy or other non-toxic shiny leaves with melted chocolate. The underside will give a more defined result.

Allow the chocolate to set, then carefully peel away the leaf from the chocolate.

Making chocolate curls

These curls can be sprinkled over almost any chocolate dish for a delicate finishing touch.

Using a block of chocolate at room temperature, draw a vegetable peeler across the block. Vary the length of the scrapes to make shorter or longer curls.

Published by Murdoch Books® a division of Murdoch Magazines Pty Limited, 45 Jones Street, Ultimo NSW 2007.

Murdoch Books and Le Cordon Bleu thank the 32 masterchefs of all the Le Cordon Bleu Schools, whose knowledge and expertise have made this book possible, especially: Chef Cliche (MOF), Chef Terrien, Chef Boucheret, Chef Duchêne (MOF), Chef Guillut, Chef Steneck, Paris; Chef Males, Chef Walsh, Chef Hardy, London; Chef Chantefort, Chef Bertin, Chef Jambert, Chef Honda, Tokyo; Chef Salembien, Chef Boutin, Chef Harris, Sydney; Chef Lawes, Adelaide; Chef Guiet, Chef Denis, Ottawa. Of the many students who helped the Chefs test each recipe, a special mention to graduates David Welch and Allen Wertheim. A very special acknowledgment to Directors Susan Eckstein, Great Britain, and Kathy Shaw, Paris, who have been responsible for the coordination of the Le Cordon Bleu team throughout this series.

Murdoch Books®
Managing Editor: Kay Halsey
Series Concept, Design and Art Direction: Juliet Cohen
Editor: Justine Upex
Food Director: Jody Vassallo
Food Editors: Dimitra Stais, Kathy Knudsen, Tracy Rutherford
Designer: Norman Baptista
Photographer: Chris Jones
Food Stylist: Mary Harris
Food Preparation: Christine Sheppard, Kerrie Ray
Chef's Techniques Photographer: Reg Morrison
Home Economists: Michelle Lawton, Kerrie Mullins, Kerrie Ray

CEO & Publisher: Anne Wilson
Publishing Director: Catie Ziller
General Manager: Mark Smith
Creative Director: Marylouise Brammer
International Sales Director: Mark Newman

National Library of Australia Cataloguing-in-Publication Data
Chocolate. ISBN 0 86411 740 X. 1. Cookery (Chocolate). (Series: Le Cordon Bleu home collection). 641.6374

Printed by Toppan Printing (S) Pte. Ltd.
First Printed 1998
©Design and photography Murdoch Books® 1998
©Text Le Cordon Bleu 1998

Distributed in the UK by D Services, 6 Euston Street, Freemen's Common, Leicester LE2 7SS Tel 0116-254-7671 Fax 0116-254-4670. Distributed in Canada by Whitecap (Vancouver) Ltd, 351 Lynn Avenue, North Vancouver, BC V7J 2C4 Tel 604-980-9852 Fax 604-980-8197 or Whitecap (Ontario) Ltd, 47 Coldwater Road, North York, ON M3B 1Y8 Tel 416-444-3442 Fax 416-444-6630

The Publisher and Le Cordon Bleu wish to thank Carole Sweetnam for her help with this series.
Front cover: Truffle torte.

IMPORTANT INFORMATION

CONVERSION GUIDE

1 cup = 250 ml (8 fl oz)
1 Australian tablespoon = 20 ml (4 teaspoons)
1 UK tablespoon = 15 ml (3 teaspoons)

NOTE: We have used 20 ml tablespoons. If you are using a 15 ml tablespoon, for most recipes the difference will be negligible. For recipes using baking powder, gelatine, bicarbonate of soda and flour, add an extra teaspoon for each tablespoon specified.

CUP CONVERSIONS—DRY INGREDIENTS

1 cup flour, plain or self-raising = 125 g (4 oz)
1 cup sugar, caster = 250 g (8 oz)
1 cup breadcrumbs, dry = 125 g (4 oz)

IMPORTANT: Those who might be at risk from the effects of salmonella food poisoning (the elderly, pregnant women, young children and those suffering from immune deficiency diseases) should consult their GP with any concerns about eating raw eggs.